Again everything seemed like an eternity, but it had only been seconds since the battle had begun. Suddenly out of the enraging battle Amigo emerged bleeding heavily from the right side of his head. His right ear looked to be ripped, shredded and torn by the razor sharp claws of the dangerous cougar.

Amigo

by **Ray Lloyd**

ISBN: 1-4782-2065-1
ISBN-13: 9781478220657

Dedicated to my daughter Kristi,
my son Michael,
my daughter Kelly,
her husband Geoff,
and my grandson Griffin,
all of whom I love very much.

Chapter 1

No one knew for sure, but according to the veterinarian that administered the protective immunizations Amigo was a Siberian husky/wolf hybrid who was probably born in the month of June 1982.

Nothing is known about Amigo's first nine months of existence and one can only guess. Judging from his behavior and character, the animal had experienced both affection and abuse. One thing is known for sure, Amigo was a very aggressive and extremely intelligent animal. This is where the story begins.

Jack Simms was a local tough who had a well deserved reputation for drinking, brawling and having a very unsavory disposition. Most of the people in town suspected Jack guilty of a lot more than just being a town bully.

Jack usually could be seen driving around town in his recently acquired dark blue 4x4 pick-up truck. You couldn't help but notice the shiny chrome roll bar, spotlight attached, adorning the rugged hooligan's vehicle. It was the type of truck lots of young people drove, but when you looked at Jack's truck, you also noticed at least one or two dogs he kept on short chains in the bed of the pick-up.

Folks thought it was bad enough to drive around with dogs loose in the back of a truck, but chaining the animals was even worse. These dogs were unusually large and tended to be vicious in nature or at the very least, on the aggressive side. The dogs never appeared to be the same animals over any period of time. Folks suspected Simms of stealing these animals to stage dogfights in neighboring towns or out in the desert. No one could prove it; and if anyone knew anything they weren't talking knowing Jack Simms to be the bully he was.

One night, Sgt Jared Walker of the county Sheriff's Department was on a stake-out at a cheap run down motel on the outskirts of town. Recently there seemed to be a large increase in drug trafficking, and the owner of the motel was under suspicion.

Sgt. Walker had been with the Sheriff's Department the last 12 years, having started as a reserve officer soon after he and his wife, Joyce, were married. Jared Walker was known to be a kind man, a nice man to all. He was tall, lean and slender but solid and stronger than one would expect. His square jaw, dark eyes and thick black hair gave him somewhat of a younger appearance than his 42 years.

Sgt. Walker had relieved another deputy at midnight. He settled in for his shift keeping a keen eye on the suspicious motel. As it so happened, it turned out to be a very quiet night. Only two vehicles entered the parking lot all night and both of them arrived sometime within the first hour of the stake-out. Evidently they had taken rooms for the night and both appeared to be legitimate. Sgt. Walker continued the detailed stake-out without incident. Just as his shift was about to end for the night, a dark blue pick-up pulled in behind the motel office. Sgt. Walker knew the driver to be Jack Simms. He watched the young rowdy get out of the truck and walk towards the motel office. In the rear of the truck, a wolf-like appearing animal was silently watching as Simms strode away. Sgt. Walker saw nothing suspicious about the trouble-maker but continued to keep a sharp eye on the proceedings.

Suddenly without warning some startling events began to occur. Two stray dogs came frolicking down the street thrusting their noses to and fro, inspecting any and all things that seemed of interest. They stopped to investigate every garbage can they came upon. After tipping one over and shattering the peaceful quiet of the early morning, the pesky pair approached the Simms pick-up. Until now, the dog that had been sitting quietly in the back of the pick-up, suddenly jumped up, rearing on his hind legs, pulling against the chain and tried as hard as he could to break free. With hair standing on end, the wolf-like animal snarled and growled fiercely at the stray canines. Coming to the conclusion that they were not wanted, the frisky pups ran down the street as fast as their legs could carry them.

Sgt. Walker sat still continuing the stake-out all the while contemplating the noisy confrontation he had just witnessed. He was impressed by the exuberance and spirit of the animal in Jack Simms' pick-up. He had given thought of acquiring just such of dog.

Two months ago, he and his wife had purchased a small ranch a few miles out of town. They thought it would be a perfect place to raise their two young children.

Although the Walker family already had two dogs and a horse, Jared felt this dog could be a beneficial addition to the family. The watchdog he thought of acquiring. Sgt. Walker decided to ask Jack Simms if he was willing to sell the dog, providing the animal was not vicious or a danger to anyone.

Jared noting his shift had come to an end, got out of the car and ambled slowly towards the dark blue pick-up.

The dog was sitting completely still and watched intently as Sgt. Walker approached. Aware of the placidness of the animal, Jared extended his right hand towards the dog and whispered gently, "Hello, big fella, how are you?"

The canine responded by slowly wagging his tail and began licking the offered hand. The dog appeared to enjoy the attention this stranger expressed.

About this time, Jack Simms returned and greeted Jared with an unfriendly: "What's going on here?"

Although Jared knew Jack and his reputation, Simms did not know Sgt. Walker well enough to recognize him. Jared motioned towards the dog sitting patiently in the truck and inquired, "Are you interested in selling your dog?"

Simms replied. "He's a pretty good and valuable dog," scratching his head, he continued. "I dunno, I dunno, how much you figure on givin' for him?"

Sgt. Walker pondered for a moment and agreed. "Yes, he certainly is a beautiful animal and I need a good watchdog. Why don't you tell me how much you have to have for him."

Jack began scratching his head again, paused a moment, then finally spoke. "I'll take $150.00 for 'em, not a penny less."

Jared didn't hesitate and could hear himself declaring, "Alright, it's a deal," then as an afterthought asked, "By the way, where did you get him and what breed is he?"

Simms didn't seem surprised by the inquiries and told Jared he had found the dog running loose a few miles from town out in the desert. He said the animal was in ragged condition, hungry, thirsty and in need of care. Simms stated, after giving the dog food and drink, he took him to a veterinarian and had him looked after. The doctor expressed that the dog was a Siberian husky/wolf hybrid. Simms went on to tell Jared about an ad he had placed in the lost and found section of the classifieds. He said he had run the ad for one week without any response.

Jared accepted Jack's explanation, thought it believable and paid him the money agreed upon. To be on the safe side Jared made a mental note to check out Jack's story.

Simms had a short rope he had taken from the pick-up and tied it to the dog's collar. Upon handing the makeshift leash to Jared, Jack said on parting, "Don't know his name, I just call him Dog, so you can call him whatever suits you."

Sgt. Walker thanked him and took the dog to his car. The canine happily jumped into the backseat and sat down.

Chapter 2

On the way home Jared decided to stop by the newspaper office and check out Jack Simms explanation concerning the ad.

The lady at the classified desk pushed a few tabs on the computer and in less than a minute verified that Jack Simms had run such an ad.

Since he was already there, Sgt. Walker thought it would be a good idea to put an ad in the paper protecting himself in case something unexpected came up. The ad read:

Found: SIBERIAN HUSKY/WOLF HYBRID
call TW3-9897 and identify.

The ad was to run the following week. Having finished his business at the newspaper office, Jared headed home to wife and family. As he was turning into the driveway, Sgt. Walker reflected on his wife and children and how they would accept the arrival of the new member of their family.

Jared had been concerned about his wife Joyce, his son Jimmy and his daughter Julie, living so far from town.

With the three being alone when he was working the night shift, Jared thought a good watchdog would create a safe environment for his family.

The two dogs now owned by the Walkers, Duke and Dudley had been with the family the past seven years and were usually just a pair of loafers. Duke was a collie/shepherd mix and Dudley was mostly Labrador retriever. Although they were large dogs, both spent most of their time enjoying the sun or shade. At either rate, they always could be found lying on the soft green carpet of grass that embellished the Walker ranch.

Joyce was sitting on the front porch relaxing and could see Jared was not alone. She became a little puzzled when she saw Jared with a dog in the backseat of the car.

Jared stopped the vehicle, got out and opened the rear door and shouted to Joyce, "Meet the new addition to our family."

In the ensuing moments everything happened so fast that Joyce didn't get a chance to respond. Jared had taken a grip on the rope and was bringing the new pet out of the car. At the same time Duke and Dudley came around the corner of the house running to greet their master. The children were presently out on the porch with their mother. No one was prepared for the clamor and commotion that was about to begin.

The new arrival lunged wildly at the two friendly dogs, almost pulling Jared off his feet. The Sgt. reacted quickly, keeping a firm grasp on the rope, holding his growling, snarling ball of fire in check. Duke and Dudley teamed up and began to bark and growl in return. Joyce was shouting and the kids with hands covering their ears and holding their heads were also shouting. One never heard such pandemonium in all one's life. Jared was startled and moving swiftly returned the rankled canine to the backseat of the car. Then he joined the children and Joyce standing on the front porch.

Jared knew Joyce was a woman with the patience of Job, nevertheless he could tell by looking into her eyes that he had some explaining to do. He also knew it better be good. Meanwhile, Duke and Dudley retreated to the backyard and the usual peace and quiet of the ranch returned.

Joyce standing rigid, her arms folded and eyes fixed, asked in a calm but cool voice. "Well, can we all hear what you and your hairy friend have to say for yourselves?"

Jared lowered his head to hide the smile showing on his face. He was aware that smile would really get him in trouble. Then he told them the whole story to the present time. He continued in detail how this dog would be a good watchdog and how he felt the family would be safer with such a pugnacious animal.

After hearing the offered explanation, but far from being convinced, Joyce relented and said. "We'll see, we shall see."

Later in the day after wondering a great deal about what had transpired, Jared was positive he knew part of the problem. He placed Duke and Dudley in the garage so he could put his notions to the test. Then with Joyce and the children in tow, they approached the car. Jared opened the door and the dog jumped out with his tail wagging and greeted the children. He began to lick their extended hands. Then begging more affection the dog leaned gently against Joyce.

Joyce stood seemingly inflexible with her arms tightly folded about her. Finally she relented and stroked the affectionate animal. She then asked, "What's his name?"

Jared replied, "He doesn't have a name, Simms just called him Dog."

Joyce thought a moment, then offered. "Well, I have a name for him."

"What's that?" Jared asked.

"Trouble, call him Trouble." Joyce echoed.

Jimmy and Julie began laughing and all agreed, Trouble was an excellent choice of names.

The experiment was only half over. Jared asked Julie to get a leash and bring Dudley out. At the same time he had taken a solid grip on the rope that was still attached to the now amiable Trouble.

It turned out to be just as Jared had expected it would. When Julie led Dudley into view, bedlam broke out as before. Trouble struggled to break free from the grasp of the rope that Jared was holding tightly. Trouble growled loudly and became extremely combative. Julie immediately returned Dudley to the garage and there was peace once again. The answer had become quite apparent. Trouble accepted and enjoyed human companionship but had little or no use for his own kind.

Now the Walker family had a problem they were not expecting. With three dogs and one that was definitely antisocial, the family was placed in a unfavorable predicament.

After a lengthy family discussion they decided they would give Trouble a couple of weeks to show some improvement. Duke and Dudley were to have their freedom on the ranch, while Trouble would be separated from the friendlier pair. He would be kept in a pen which was not in use as there wasn't any need to keep Duke and Dudley under control. Jared was hoping Trouble would become more acquainted with the surroundings and maybe his attitude would change for the better.

As it turned out the Walker family was doing a lot of wishful thinking, not only was Trouble hostile towards Duke and Dudley, he just didn't like any four legged animal. The family's beautiful Appaloosa mare, Stardust, also became a target of his dissidence.

During the second week of Trouble's stay at the ranch, Jimmy took him out for some exercise. Suddenly Duke and Dudley appeared out of nowhere. Trouble was too strong for

Jimmy and broke free of his grasp and attacked the docile pair. Sgt. Walker was working the day shift and Joyce had the task of restoring order before any of the embattled received any serious injuries.

Joyce did this quickly by latching on to the leash and gaining control over Trouble. Then she scolded him furiously.

When Jared came home that evening, Joyce told him about the incident. She added that something had to be done before one of the animals received a serious injury. Jared assured Joyce that he would try and find another home for the troublesome canine. Although he didn't want this to occur, he knew Joyce was right. Jared reiterated that he thought Trouble needed more time to adjust to the surroundings. Jared could tell by the look on her face, Joyce didn't agree and the matter was closed.

The next day when Jared arrived at the Sheriff's Department, he started to make the inquiries as he had promised Joyce. Most of his co-workers already had dogs and when Jared told of Trouble's aggressive nature, any interest shown was soon lost. One deputy, however, Larry Winters, told Jared about a friend who was a retired deputy that might be interested. This friend was about to embark on a gold mining venture throughout the western states for the next few years. Larry went on explaining how the friend, Pete Mitchell by name, had become blind in his right eye and had only partial sight in his left. Pete, now a prospector, could use a good dog for companionship and from the sound of it, this dog would make a perfect companion considering the possible dangers he may face.

Jared was happy to hear about Pete and got his phone number from Larry. Jared was going to do his best to convince Joyce to relent and give Trouble one more chance.

Upon his arrival at the ranch, Jared was pleased to find Joyce in a pleasant mood and went to work on her right away. Much to his surprise Joyce gave in and agreed to one more and the very last chance for Trouble to shape up.

That evening, Jared told Joyce and the children about Pete Mitchell. While this pleased Joyce, it saddened the children. They had already become attached to Trouble and they didn't want to lose him. When Jared explained that Trouble would not be given away unless he caused another major disturbance, Jimmy and Julie cheered up. Jared thought this would be a good time to teach the kids a lesson about allegiance. He told them that Duke and Dudley were tried and true friends. He offered that Trouble was a new acquaintance and a person doesn't turn his or her back on trusted friends. Julie and Jimmy understood and agreed.

The next few days proved to be uneventful. The animals had been separated successfully and everything around the ranch was peaceful.

That was the calm before the storm. During the 4th week at his new home, somehow, someway, Trouble managed to free himself from the pen and get loose. As luck would have it, this was Jared's day off and he was near the barn when a canine donnybrook broke out. Before Jared could gain control of the situation and bring the battle to a halt, Dudley had been nipped on his left hind leg and was limping. Jared got a solid grip on Trouble's collar and ordered Duke out of the melee and put Trouble back in the pen. The bite was not serious and Dudley had already begun to walk and run normally. This unpleasant altercation was a ticket sending Trouble to a new home. Jared telephoned Pete Mitchell within the hour.

Chapter 3

Although he wasn't leaving for at least two weeks, Pete was busy checking and preparing his mining equipment and camping gear when the telephone rang.

"Hello." Pete answered.

"Hello," was the reply from the caller. "This is Jared Walker. A mutual friend of ours, Larry Winters told me you were looking for a good dog. Is that true?"

"It sure is," a cheerful Pete Mitchell blurted and went on, "Yes siree, Larry said you might be calling. He told me about your problem with the dog and I've been anxious to hear from you."

"Well," Jared drawled, "When would be a good time to bring him by?"

"I'll be home all day."

"Fine. How does an hour from now sound to you?" Jared asked.

"I'll be looking for you." Pete replied.

Pete then gave Jared the address and directions to his home. He was extremely happy about meeting his potential companion.

As soon as he was off the phone, Pete returned to the mining equipment and continued to check and recheck the items to be taken on the trip. He was anxious before Jared called, but now with the possibility of a companero, excitement was stirring inside him.

It was almost an hour to the minute when Jared pulled into Pete's driveway. Pete was looking through the front room window. He immediately spied the large wolfish dog standing on the backseat of the car. A beaming smile shown on Pete's face as he raced out to greet his guests.

As they introduced themselves, Jared saw that Pete Mitchell was a tall and slender man like himself but somewhat older. Pete had gray hair and a gray mustache and one couldn't help but notice the black patch covering his right eye. His face, bronzed from the desert sun and wind featured high cheekbones and minor creases at the corners of his mouth and eyes. A few lines shown across his forehead. All in all and upon close study, a kind and gentle man in Jared's judgement.

Jared allowed Trouble to leave the car and Pete reached out to pet the good looking canine. The dog responded with a thorough licking of the outstretched hand.

Pete commented. "I can't believe this dog has a mean bone in his body."

"Well, I don't understand him either, but when he encounters any four legged animal, he becomes entirely unfriendly to say the least." Jared scratching his chin, sighed and spoke on. "It sure beats me, but having the three other animals on the ranch, I have to think of their safety." Jared added quickly, "He's all yours if you want him."

"Want him? Well, I sure do. What are you asking for him?"

Jared stated firmly, "Nothing, don't you worry about that. As long as he's with someone who appreciates him and will give him care and attention, I'm happy to let you have him." Jared added, "Just make sure you hang onto him when other animals are nearby. Let me know how he's doing. Drop me a short note if you get a chance. I named him Trouble but I'm sure you can find a suitable name for him."

After shaking hands, Jared got back in his car and said, "Good luck to you both."

Pete waved goodbye and assured Jared that he would write sometime during the coming summer.

Chapter 4

Pete glanced down at his new pet that was waiting patiently while continuing to wag his tail.

Pete quipped, "You're not going to be any trouble to me, are you? I'll tell you what Pardner. I've thought of a real good name for you. C'mon, Amigo, C'mon, let's go in the house and get acquainted."

The dog readily obeyed and followed Pete into his home. Pete and Amigo spent most of the day exercising and getting to know each other. Pete quickly learned to react when another dog appeared or approached. Pete would change their direction to avoid coming in contact with another animal. Pete would simultaneously speak in a gentle voice, repeating the word "easy" over and over. The soft tone of his voice calmed Amigo somewhat and the dog would not strain against the hand held leash.

The next few days were spent quietly with Pete and Amigo rapidly growing fond of each other.

Between their frequent walks Pete taught Amigo a few tricks. First he taught Amigo to fetch the leash when he wanted to go out. Then he taught the dog some fun tricks.

These were the usual tricks. Easy ones, such as shaking hands, rolling over, playing dead and how to hold food on his nose until he was allowed to have it. Pete only had to show the trick a few times and Amigo would perform flawlessly.

Only a week was left for Pete to get everything in order for the coming adventure. Pete owned a 1963 Ford pick-up truck that was as dependable as could be. It was in excellent shape and Pete was quite proud of its condition. The old vehicle had seen its share of mountain and desert trails and always remained reliable. Besides being a means of transportation, the pick-up was going to serve as a home to the wandering pair for a long time. The pick-up bed was thoroughly covered with carpet and foam cushions were placed on top. Then a sleeping bag was placed over all, making a soft and comfortable place to sleep. A camper shell was fitted snugly to the bed to keep out the rain, sleet, hail and snow. They were sure to encounter all kinds of weather on their adventure. Pete had to pack everything just right so it would all fit and still have room for himself and Amigo.

Although Pete had plenty of chores to finish before leaving, he managed to spend a lot of time exercising and playing with Amigo. The bond between the two had already become quite strong and every morning Amigo would come into Pete's bedroom and nuzzle him gently. Pete learned later that this was a normal and common greeting among wolves.

Amigo was providing a lot of companionship for his master. His intelligence was obvious and he could be very funny too.

One day Pete was lying on the sofa getting some needed rest when Amigo with his leash in tow, dropped it on his chest. Pete told Amigo to lie down and he would walk him later. Amigo growled softly and began to push Pete's arm with his nose. When this didn't get any reaction, Amigo brought Pete's shoes to him and started tossing them in the air. Pete laughed so much, he forgot he was tired and ended up taking Amigo for a walk after all.

Amigo

Amigo was a loyal and loving pet with a fondness for people, especially children. But, Pete couldn't understand why he became so belligerent when he encountered other animals. Pete pondered some and he was worried about a possible confrontation. Such a meeting could involve serious consequences. Pete had high expectations that Amigo would use his intelligence in any given situation.

As each day passed Pete and Amigo grew more and more familiar with each other. It was really uncanny, something like mental telepathy.

Today was Friday and on Monday they would be jumping into the old pick-up to begin their journey into gold and God's country. There were still the last minute details Pete had to attend to. He had to call the utility companies to make sure all services would be disconnected the day of departure. Sometime during the weekend he loaded the truck with equipment and supplies.

Pete had been growing more and more anxious as the time of departure neared. He was sure Amigo would love and enjoy the wilderness and most of all the freedom to run and roam at will. Placer gold mining could be a lonesome and dangerous undertaking. With the acquisition of Amigo the hazards had been lessened.

In addition to loading the pick-up, Pete and Amigo spent Saturday and Sunday taking walks and paying last minute goodbye visits to friends and relatives.

On Sunday Pete telephoned Sgt. Walker at the Sheriff's Department to let him know how Amigo was improving. Jared was happy to hear that Amigo's aggressive behavior appeared to have diminished somewhat. But he did show some concern about the possibilities of confrontations in the wild.

Pete reassured Jared that he would write a letter informing him of Amigo's progress. Pete finished the conversation by telling Jared how Amigo came by his name.

Chapter 5

It was 5 A.M. Monday when Pete jumped out of bed.

Amigo was still sleeping and Pete began to shave and realized this would be the last hot water shave and shower he would have for a long time. As Pete finished brewing a pot of coffee, Amigo started to stretch and loosen up. Moments later, he nuzzled up to Pete greeting him the same way he did every morning. After a couple of cups of black coffee, he took Amigo out for a walk. Then he filled a thermos bottle with the remaining coffee and began carrying items to the pick-up truck.

Pete had loaded the truck carefully putting in gear that would not be needed until a permanent camp could be set up. Then he worked his way towards the tailgate placing two coolers with food and drink last. Every night until permanently camped, he would have to jostle equipment and supplies around to permit room for himself and Amigo to sleep. This was the middle of April and Pete knew there was a lot of bad weather ahead of them. He was hoping to take advantage of the heavy winter snowstorms. The spring run-offs would more than likely move new gold into the creeks, streams and rivers.

It was 9 A.M. when Pete rolled out of the driveway and headed towards the highway that would take them north into the gold country. Amigo sitting next to Pete didn't miss a thing as he turned his head to and fro viewing everything in sight. Seemingly the canine knew an exciting trip was in the making. Finally as Pete drove the old truck out of town and into the desert Amigo settled down and lay quietly on the seat.

Like many people who have driven down a lonely highway, Pete began to daydream. He started thinking of past mining ventures and wondered how this one would compare to the others. Due to his poor eye condition, he had sold his 5 inch gold dredge following his doctors orders. His doctor absolutely had forbidden Pete to work underwater. Now it was back to the basic pick, shovel, sluicebox, buckets, gold pan and a lot of old fashioned hard work. Pete looked over at Amigo who was quietly taking a nap. He smiled at his new companion aware that this was going to be some journey.

The first day on the road Amigo probably saw cattle for the very first time. As they passed by a herd close to the highway, Pete had to reach out and grab Amigo's collar to keep him from trying to break through the windshield.

Pete scolded Amigo. "Lay down and behave. Those critters aren't doing you any harm. You just lay down."

Amigo didn't lie down, instead he sat down with an anxious look on his face anticipating more excitement.

They were leaving the desert and approaching the Sierra Nevada mountains and the weather was substantially cooler now. Snow covered the higher elevations and the mountains overlooking the desert were majestic.

They had been traveling just a little over three hours and Pete figured they would take Tioga Pass through Yosemite National Park to the west side of the Sierras. They would have plenty of daylight to set up camp and still have time to do some limited prospecting.

The terrain was changing rapidly to a rich forest green as they continued northward. It wasn't long before a handsome mule deer trotted slowly across the highway, then not long after, a gray wily coyote raced across the barren road and disappeared quickly into the tall trees and brush. Amigo responded to both animals exactly in the same way as he had to the previous herd of cattle.

Pete shook his head, looked at Amigo and spoke in a calm voice. "We're just going to have to adjust your attitude, my Amigo."

Amigo with his tongue hanging over his jowls, resumed his anxious watch and remained alert searching the roadside.

The first big disappointment of the journey came when Pete turned off the main highway and onto the road that was to take them over Tioga Pass. A large orange and black sign appeared informing Pete that the pass was closed due to the heavy snows. This was a serious set-back because now they had to continue northward and that meant cold and inclement weather to contend with. They could back track 100 miles or so but that idea was quickly discarded. It was only a minute or two and they were back on the highway driving into unpredictable weather. As they drove on Amigo continued to search and scan looking through the truck window for any sign of movement which may cause some excitement.

Pete's earlier suspicion of possible bad weather proved to be right on the money. Within the hour he was guiding the pick-up through a heavy wet snowfall. He immediately began to look for a good place to camp for the night. Amigo was about to experience snow for the very first time and as if in anticipation, his tail seemed to move back in forth in time with the wiper blades.

Pete soon found a suitable campsite sheltered by huge pine trees with plenty of firewood lying about. He quickly started a fire and after some hot coffee and chicken soup he and Amigo began to work and play. Pete doing the work, Amigo having a wonderful time playing in the snow.

Pete busied himself gathering enough firewood to last the night and furnish a hot breakfast in the morning. He took time to watch and enjoy Amigo and his antics. Amigo was now free to run and roam at will. He was having the time of his life romping in the freshly fallen snow.

After watching Amigo finally exhaust himself, Pete prepared the back of the truck for sleeping. He made sure the fire was burning brightly, furnishing some comfortable heat.

Pete slowly drifted off to sleep wondering what the next day would bring. He now had to change his plans as they were some 100 miles north and east of where he had planned to be. Now a new destination was in order. Amigo was sound asleep as darkness came and filled the night as the snow continued to fall. The first day of the journey had come to an end.

Pete was awakened by Amigo's cold nosed greeting shortly after 6 A.M. The snow had stopped falling sometime during the night and the campfire was still showing some sign of life. Smoke was rising slowly into the air only to disappear into the tall pines. After a few cups of hot black coffee, Pete covered the fire with snow, loaded the truck and they were back on the road by 8 A.M. As he did the day before, Amigo assumed his watchful position.

It was a bright sunny day and Pete knew of a claim he could work about 70 miles to the northwest. He could see snow on the mountain tops in every direction. Down at the lower levels the weather was pleasant enough to sluice and since the claim was situated in a small canyon there wouldn't be any snow to contend with. Pete had found a small amount of flour gold there a few years back and decided to try his luck once more.

It was somewhere around mid-morning when Pete and Amigo arrived at the logging road that would take them to the claim. Eleven miles of rough and winding road, up the mountain, down the mountain, switchback after switchback before finally reaching the campsite and claim. The fact that it was early spring made travel into the canyons dangerous. A person had to worry about mud and rock slides occurring and the possibility of being trapped and having to walk for help. Pete was well aware of the situation and he proceeded very carefully.

They arrived at the claim about an hour later after a rough and bumpy ride. Amigo jumped out of the pick-up and immediately began to sniff every bush, rock and tree in the area. Pete was pleased that his companion was happy.

With intense curiosity, Amigo continued to investigate everything in sight. Pete began to unload the pick-up placing the equipment in the proper places for easy access.

Meanwhile Amigo had seen a perky chipmunk and quickly gave chase only to see the little rodent disappear into a hole beneath an old rotten stump. Pete noticed the bewildered look on Amigo's face as the chipmunk vanished.

Chapter 6

After setting up the camp Pete enjoyed a cold drink along with some potato salad and roasted hot dogs with all the trimmings. Upon sniffing the odor of the juicy hot dogs Amigo forgot the chipmunks and ground squirrels and began to pester his master for dinner.

The claim belonged to a friend Pete had placered with in the past. Pete had his pals permission to work the claim anytime he cared to. The U.S. Forest Service had run some tests several years ago leaving some deep excavations.

This left huge piles of dirt and rock near the stream that could easily be worked.

Having eaten a good lunch and filled with anxiety Pete began scouting the creek. He sought out the best place to set up the sluicebox. After placing the sluice in the stream Pete gathered some 5 gallon buckets, a pick and shovel and began digging. When the buckets were three quarters full Pete carried them down to the sluice and emptied the contents into the box. This method of mining is called high banking and is usually successful. It's also hard and backbreaking work. Approximately four hours later Pete cleaned out the sluicebox, placed the concentrates in a bucket, then panned out the gold. The first day results were meager, no nuggets were to be found, only some fines and some flakes shone in the pan.

Pete was well aware there would be many days such as this and probably more with even less color.

Sometime during the night Pete was awakened by the sound of raindrops splashing loudly on the aluminum campershell. He slowly went back to sleep hoping the rain would cease by morning light. Not only did the rain fall all night, it continued to pour and drizzle for the next three days and nights. At times the rain would turn into sleet and sometime the sleet would become a wet snow. The weather was miserable and Pete and Amigo had to stay in the pick-up or under a canvas shelter. Pete had built a temporary leanto between some pine trees for just such a reason. Pete kept a continuous small fire going at one end of the protected area which enabled the pair to keep warm and enjoy hot food and drink whenever needed. With all things considered Pete and Amigo kept dry and comfortable under the inclement conditions.

When the onslaught of water finally stopped Pete and Amigo enjoyed a week of sunny and warm weather.

Pete worked hard that week but the results were scanty. He figured he had less than 3 pennyweight of gold to show for all his efforts. This amounted to less than $60.00 and he was seriously thinking about moving on.

Between his numerous naps Amigo kept busy chasing chipmunks and ground squirrels. Although he had the freedom to run at will Amigo often approached Pete with the red leash hanging loosely from his jaws. He still appreciated any daily walks he could coax from his master.

One day while on an exploration of the area Pete and Amigo stumbled on two tunnels leading into the side of a mountain. The first excavation and the lower of the two was almost concealed by heavy underbrush. If it was not for Amigo's constant sniffing and interest in everything new, Pete may have walked on by. Upon finding the first tunnel Pete scanned the surroundings and noticed a second opening approximately 40 feet directly above the first. His first instinct was to enter the excavations but good judgement prevailed and Pete decided to wait until the following morning.

Pete was up at the crack of dawn in anticipation of what the tunnels might have to offer. Even some relics or some old coins would cause some excitement. After a good breakfast consisting of hot cakes, eggs and bacon, washed down by some hot coffee, Pete started to gather the gear that he thought he would need. He collected his metal detector, rock hammer, flashlight and lantern. These items in addition to the mining tools he carried in his backpack would be sufficient to explore the darkened tunnels.

When the two reached the lower tunnel Pete was very cautious keeping Amigo on the leash, not knowing if any wild animals were using the excavation as a home. Amigo eagerly led the way and since he was not growling or barking Pete felt it was safe to enter.

Using the flashlight Pete scanned the walls and could see the hard rock that made up the mass of earth surrounding them. The hard rock interior assured their safety. Pete and Amigo advanced slowly deeper into the tunnel searching for a sign of any precious metal or valuable ore.

As Pete and Amigo proceeded further into the tunnel Pete thought it would be wise to light and use the gas lantern in addition to the flashlight. They only moved a few more yards when suddenly Amigo began to growl then tugged and strained against Pete's tightened grasp. Instantly Pete became alarmed and while controlling Amigo with his right hand, he lifted the lantern into the air with his left. He saw the object of Amigo's wrath just in time.

Pete shouted, "C'mon boy, let's get out of here, let's vamoose." He kept a steadfast grip on Amigo and pulled him back quickly. They retreated as fast as they could to the tunnel entrance.

They had unintentionally intruded upon a mother skunk and her newborn babies and both Pete and Amigo were about to suffer a lesson in humiliation. Luckily the small black and white animal armed with its pungent perfume was only making ready to fire away.

After reaching safety and exhaling deeply, Pete laughed and stammered, "Whew, you sure were lucky, Amigo." Amigo looked at Pete and tilted his head from side to side in wonderment as Pete was speaking.

Pete entertained the idea of excluding a trip into the second excavation but his curiosity got the best of him and soon he and Amigo were entering the other tunnel.

This cavity turned out to be much like the lower minus the unwanted inhabitants. Using his rock hammer and chisel, Pete gathered a few samples of ore, all of which turned out to be white quartz sprinkled throughout with pyrite, better known as fool's gold.

Since the morning events turned out to be an unimpressive venture, Pete returned to his regular mining activities and Amigo was soon enjoying his favorite pastime, chasing the areas numerous rodents.

The following week produced more nasty weather and it came in multiple forms, rain, sleet, snow and hail. Unable to do any work and with provisions running low Pete decided that it would be a good time to move to another claim. On the way he could stock up on groceries and supplies. That day Pete and Amigo broke camp and started towards a new location near the Oregon border.

Chapter 7

After purchasing the needed provisions and spending a good part of the day driving, Pete was relieved when he saw the logging road that would take them down into the canyon and claim. The road twisted and turned constantly with many switchbacks and Pete breathed a sigh of relief when they finally leveled off on the canyon floor. Driving along beside the river Pete waved at a miner busy tending his sluice and continued on into the canyon. There were two cabins along the river before Pete reached the claim. The cabin nearest to Pete's claim appeared to be occupied as smoke was seen rising slowly from the chimney. It was comforting to know a neighbor was close at hand.

It was now the middle of May and Pete was hoping all the cold and nasty weather was behind them. He felt renewed optimism having arrived at the new location and was anxious to resume mining as soon as possible.

Amigo was delighted with his new surroundings and there were plenty of chipmunks and the like to chase and occupy his time.

Two weeks passed by quickly and Pete was getting cabin fever. He hadn't talked to anyone during this time and the claim hadn't proved any more prosperous than the prior site. Pete was disappointed and a little depressed and thought this would be a good time to call on his neighbor.

Pete spoke to Amigo who was lying quietly in the warm sun. "Let's take a walk, big fella." Amigo was quick to respond when he saw the familiar red leash. An excited Amigo knew a walk was forthcoming. Pete attached the leash to the dog's collar and they headed down the road.

They walked slowly and Pete was speaking softly, but not about anything in particular. He was just rambling on to Amigo because he knew Amigo liked the sound of his voice. Amigo happily pranced alongside.

It was a warm and sunny day and all was serene and quiet as they walked towards the near-by cabin. The pair were within 100 yards or so of their neighbor's place when the sleepy afternoon stillness erupted into mass mayhem. A pack of ferocious barking and growling dogs surrounded Pete and Amigo.

There were three black and two white crossbreed dogs. They all were showing and flashing their teeth. After forming a semi-circle around the pair, a black moved in to attack. Pete while holding Amigo on the leash waved his free arm and yelled fiercely at the attacker.

For the moment this sent the black dog in retreat. Then another of the pack charged from the rear. Amigo whirled around and met the assailant head on sending his teeth into the dog's scruffy neck. At this instant a white cur snarling and flashing razor sharp teeth attacked Amigo's flank. Pete was still waving his arm frantically and continued to shout at the violent pack. Amigo released his grip on the neck of the dog he was holding then moving with amazing speed dodged the jaws of the white and sank his teeth into the hind quarter of the new attacker. Amigo slackened from this adversary and turned expecting to meet a foe from another direction but the warring group appeared to back off for a few moments. Now

Amigo was pulling hard trying desperately to combat the nearest of the pack. A black that seemed unsure of its brothers.

Pete had to use sufficient restraint to keep Amigo in check. The pack momentarily in retreat started closing in again. Then Pete heard someone sternly shout in a loud and deep voice.

"Mose, Corky, hyar, hyar y'all git back hyar."

Upon hearing the severe tone of the voice, the roguish canines reluctantly began to back away. A man was walking towards Pete and Amigo continuing to shout at the retreating animals. "Zeke, Sham , Pepper, git, git ya varmits, git on outta hyar."

A large man with a full black beard wearing bib overhauls and knee high rubber boots was standing between the pack of dogs and Pete and Amigo. Although he had a gruff demeanor and had just disciplined his group of rowdy brutes, there was a sparkle in his gray eyes. Smiling he spoke to Pete. "Sorree mister, ah wuzn't expectin' no one up this way. If'n ah knew, these boys wudn't been a runnin' loose. Lemme put 'em in thar pen."

After placing the dogs in their pen the man returned and extended his big hand to Pete and said, "Muh names Taylor, Jesse Taylor. That's some dawg y'all got there. Never seen the like of it. That dawg's got more sand than all my boys put together."

Pete returned the healthy handshake and replied. " Pete Mitchell, I'm glad to know you." Pete offered more. "I don't know about his sand, but I was scared as hell. We're thankful you showed up and lucky too."

"Ah wuz down at the creek tendin' muh sluice when ah heard all the ruckus. Ah got hyar as soon as ah could." Jesse was shaking his head as he again praised Amigo. " That dawg of yore's sure stands tall."

"I guess he does at that, I know I'm pretty proud of him. By the way Jesse, I'm working some diggin's up the road and that's how we happen to come along. I thought we would be neighborly but I didn't count on starting a war."

Jesse spoke apologetically. "Those boys of mine are all from the same litter, all brothers and they kinda stick together. We didn't expect any company, they'll stay in thar coop now."

Over the next few hours the two men drank coffee and talked an arm an leg off of each other. Amigo lay quietly alongside Pete during the friendly visit. Both men complained of disappointment in their diggings. While Jesse didn't have any choice, Pete could pack his gear and move on anytime he wished. He told Jesse that he was seriously thinking of moving up into Oregon.

Jesse sighed and said. "Ah hate to see ya go now that we're neighbors, but ah know how ya feel."

Shaking his head Pete answered, "Well I'll give it some thought for a few days then I'll make my decision. In the meantime, why don't you pay us a visit and let me repay your hospitality."

As their talk continued Pete and Jesse noticed that the sky was becoming darker by the minute.

Pete was the first to mention it. "It's clouding up fast. Amigo and I better get back to camp before some real nasty weather sets in."

"Shore 'nuff looks like it." Jesse remarked. "Those clouds are rollin' by quick like. Mite stur up a good storm. Mebbe some hail to boot."

As the two men said their good-byes, Jesse affectionately stroked Amigo about the head. He also assured Pete that he would stop by soon.

A few drops of rain began to fall as Pete waved his farewell and started to walk back to camp.

By the time Pete and Amigo reached their camp the rain was coming down so hard that Pete could barely see more than a few yards ahead. They both jumped into the bed of the pick-up eager to dry off and get comfortable. Pete thought about how little things like this could make such a difference. He really was living much like the people did in the mid 1800s.

As Pete lay daydreaming the storm had picked up in intensity. He was suddenly shaken back to reality when a violent, loud clap of thunder roared through the heavens. This caused his attention to observe a bolt of lightning zigzag down to earth and split the base of a pine tree less than thirty yards from the pick-up. Then just as Jesse had predicted, the clinking sound of tiny pieces of ice began to bounce off the aluminum canopy. It was hailing and it wasn't long before white beads of ice covered the earth.

Pete noticed that Amigo had become quite anxious, so he immediately began to stroke and talk to his pet. Amigo soon calmed down and got as close to Pete as possible.

The hail slowly changed into rain, sometimes coming down in torrents, sometimes falling lightly but always steady.

Soon the pitter-patter of the falling rain had led Pete into a deep but troubled sleep.

Sometime later when he awakened, Pete could only remember bits and pieces about a dream he had just had. The dream seemed to be some kind of warning. Something inside him was telling him to be alert and careful in the future.

Chapter 8

A few days passed without any more inclement weather. Even though it was only the middle of June, it was hotter than usual during the day. The nights were still brisk and cool. Pete was down at the river loading gravel into five gallon buckets to be carried and run through the sluicebox. Since his labors hadn't produced much color, his thoughts were running toward leaving if things didn't improve.

Amigo was taking a daily swim and cooling off in a hole that had been dredged out in years gone by. Amigo liked the water and visited his private swimming pool two or three times a day.

Pete had filled two 5 gallon buckets and was carrying them to the sluice when he heard a husky voice call out.

"Hullo Pete, do ya need any help with all that gold yore a totin'?"

Pete looked up from the steep river bank to see Jesse standing near a big pine and answered, "I'd about given up on you."

As soon as Amigo heard Jesse's voice he was out of the water. Wagging his tail joyfully, he ran quickly towards the big friendly man.

Pete placed the containers on the ground and walked up the river bank to greet Jesse and invite him to some coffee and cookies.

The two men shook hands and Jesse gave Amigo a few pats on his head. You could see a twinkle in his eyes as he spoke. "This ol' man shore 'nuff snuck up on y'all."

Pete agreed but jokingly laid all the blame on Amigo. "Yeah, you better wake up, big guy. I might have to farm you out."

Jesse laughed. "Just send 'im down to muh spread anytime ya want."

Back at camp, Pete brewed coffee, then he and Jesse sat and talked. Jesse explained to Pete why he hadn't dropped by sooner. It seems the wind and hail had caused some damage to his cabin. He had spent the last few days making repairs. Then as Jesse finished his story about the storm damage, his face took on a worried frown and he spoke in earnest. "Pete, thar's a big cat pokin' his nose hereabouts. Me un the boys trailed em aways yes'tidy. We lost the critter up on the mountain. The last day er two that cat's been a sneak'in 'roun muh place. Ya know those cats usually stay clear of humin's but this un is actin' a bit queer like. Anyways, y'all be a mite careful an stay on yore toes. If ya got a shootin' iron, I'd pack it if'n ah wuz you." Jesse nodded and pointed toward a fir tree off to his right.

With this gesture, Pete looked and saw a 30-30 carbine leaning against the tree.

Jesse continued to speak, but still on a somber note. "Mite not be nothin' to fret about, mebbe nothin' a'tall. That ol' catamount mite have left by now, but ah thought it a good idee to warn y'all. See'un yore dawg the way ah do, ah don't reckon he'd back off. Amigo could get hurt, hurt bad, er even wurse."

Pete nodded and answered. "Thanks Jesse, I do have a .38 snub nose revolver I keep for protection. I have never had to use it and I sure hope I never do, and you're right about Amigo.

I'm sure he would take on any critter and I have worried a lot about such an incident occurring. Not only have I given thought about him meeting up with a cougar or a bear, but I've worried about rattler's, porky's and even skunks. I don't want him tangling with any wild animal but he has that instinct to hunt and I like giving him his free rein. He usually stays pretty close to me but every so often he goes off somewhere. Darned if I know where, but there are times when he's gone for an hour or more." Pete took a deep breath and continued. "Anyway Jesse, I guess Amigo and I will be pulling up stakes soon. This here ground has probably been worked out. Hardly any color of any size has shown, so I'm thinking of moving on in a few days."

"Sorree to hear that Pete, but ah know whut yore sayin' an ah can't say as ah blame ya. Don't y'all forgit to stop an say good-bye afore ya go. Speakin' of goin', ah better git back to the boys an muh diggin's, muhself. Don't forgit whut ah've tole ya 'bout that ol' catamount."

Pete shook his head in agreement and the two men shook hands and Jesse started back towards his cabin.

Considering Jesse's warning Pete sought out his .38 Smith and Wesson. After making sure the gun was loaded, he strapped it on and hoped there wouldn't be any need of it.

Chapter 9

Two days had passed since Jesse had paid his visit to Pete and Amigo. There hadn't been any sign of the mountain lion and Pete decided it wasn't really necessary to carry the revolver anymore. Not only was he confident that Amigo would give him advance warning, but he felt he was never that far away from camp.

It was Friday and Pete decided to continue to work the claim through the weekend. He would break camp on Monday, then he wouldn't have to drive in the heavy weekend traffic.

Pete was engaged in his work but at the same time was in deep thought. He was pondering on his destination into Oregon. There were good diggin's nearby in south-western Oregon, but he finally decided on traveling to northeast central Oregon, near Baker City. He had a good reason. Although he hadn't planned on reaching that location until late summer, the convincing factor was a standing invitation from a wartime buddy who had a large claim some twenty miles west of Baker City.

Amigo interrupted Pete gaining his attention by gently taking Pete's arm in his jaws and tugging lightly. Amigo began to turn around, making two or three quick circles. At first this didn't concern Pete because this was a regular occurrence when Amigo wanted to go for a walk. However, there seemed to be a difference this time. After Amigo repeated the sequence, he ran a few feet away only to return and go through the same antics again. Pete reasoned that Amigo wanted him to follow. Pete motioned with his hand indicating to Amigo to lead the way. Amigo slowly began to run in front of Pete. He would look back often to make sure Pete was following. Amigo maintained a 40 to 50 foot distance in front of Pete. Having followed Amigo approximately 10 or 12 minutes, Pete saw that Amigo had stopped and was looking down at the ground. When Pete reached the location he discovered a large hole. The excavation was similar to the test holes the Forest Service usually dug.

Pete laughed and while still smiling, asked Amigo. "What's going on, do you think there's gold down there? C'mon big fella, let me get back to work."

As Pete turned to head back, Amigo growled, and again he tugged at Pete's arm pulling Pete closer to the hole. After releasing his grip, Amigo barked and looked back into the hole. This time Pete peered into the abyss and much to his amazement saw a small trembling fawn standing in the bottom of the excavation.

Pete praised Amigo and gave him a big hug and said, "Good dog, big guy, good boy. "

Amigo stood still and looked down at the fawn acting like a proud parent. He glanced up at Pete and accepted the praise.

The hole was deep enough that Pete knew he had to get a rope to rescue the fawn. Not wanting to waste any time, he immediately started towards camp with Amigo following close behind. While taking about 10 minutes or so to reach the young deer, it only took half that time to return to camp.

Amigo appeared to be impatient while Pete was finding a rope strong enough to lower himself into the excavation. He also wanted to find a smaller line to lift the fawn up and out of the hole. Upon locating the right set of ropes needed in the rescue, Pete and Amigo set out to come to the aid of the timid deer.

Returning to the scene of the mishap, Pete couldn't help but wonder why Amigo was like a Dr. Jekyll and Mr. Hyde. He was so belligerent and aggressive towards some animals, yet was very gentle and caring with others, especially the young. Pete and Amigo hurried to the excavation holding the fawn. While it seemed like an eternity it had only been 20 minutes since they had last seen the young deer.

As Pete and Amigo approached the location, Amigo began to growl and he started to run. Soon he was barking loudly as he was full speed into his run.

Pete tried his best to keep up but soon lost sight of his pet. Pete ran as fast as he could and tried to imagine what had set Amigo off. It didn't take but another minute and he knew the answer.

There on one side of the large hole was Amigo. He was ferociously growling and poised ready to attack. On the other side was the object of his anger, the largest cougar Pete had ever seen. Pete estimated the cat weighed close to a 150 pounds.

The large tawny mountain lion stood frozen in a threatening position. Its right front leg was extended with its paw held high in the air. The cat was snarling savagely and its eyes were focused on Amigo.

The fat was in the fire. This cat was hungry and Pete and Amigo had interfered with its dinner plans. This probably made the feline more of a danger.

Chapter 10

Aware that there wasn't any way that Amigo could come out unhurt in the forthcoming battle, Pete reached down to draw his revolver. He was stunned to realize he had decided earlier there wasn't any need for it. Pete felt stupid and lost all at the same time. After a few seconds of self condemnation, Pete did the only thing he could do. He began to shout loudly. "Amigo, come here boy, heel Amigo, come here." He continued to plead, "Come here Amigo, come here boy, come Amigo."

Pete knew cougars were not prone to attacking humans, but he also knew there were always the exceptions too. He continued to shout hoping Amigo would come to his side.

The courageous pet would not respond to Pete's commands and appeared intent on preventing the big cat from dining on the helpless fawn.

Pete attempted to get close to Amigo, intending to grab his collar and pull him away. As he came closer, Pete saw he was only putting Amigo in more danger as the dog's concentration on the hungry cat was broken as he neared. For the moment, the mountain lion appeared more annoyed at the presence of the intruders and was still in a defensive position. The cougar continued to snarl viciously and raise its paw. He was determined to drive off his unwanted guests.

Amigo stopped his barking, but continued to growl and started moving to the left to flank the cat. His adversary turned swiftly and faced Amigo once more. Still not ready to charge, Amigo sized up his opponent and began to circle in the other direction.

While the ensuing showdown between the angry pair was gathering momentum, Pete noticed there was another spectator besides himself. Less than 25 yards away, almost totally camouflaged by a dense thicket, stood what Pete surmised to be the worried mother of the endangered fawn. She was nervously watching the proceedings but completely helpless in the situation. She appeared determined to stay and wasn't about to abandon her offspring in its time of need.

At the same time, Pete was trying his best to think of some way to help Amigo. He remembered he had his old scout knife in his pocket and he quickly broke a suitable limb off of a nearby tree. The limb was fairly straight and close to eight feet long. As fast as he could, Pete began to whittle a sharp point on the end of the limb.

As Pete was busy fashioning the impromptu weapon, Amigo made several feint charges towards the menacing lion. It seemed he was ready to attack and drive the big cat off.

With a furious growl Amigo sprang into action. Flashing his white fangs he attacked his larger enemy with ferocious abandon.

The big cat was momentarily in surprise. It was as if he couldn't believe this lone foe would initiate an assault. The catamount leaped high in the air avoiding the canine's initial strike. He came down unscathed and ready to meet his attacker. Amigo didn't waste anytime and spun around and collided with the larger animal as the cat countered. The cougar's claws were lightning quick but still only managed a light graze and Amigo remained unhurt. The two animals were moving so fast that it was hard to follow their movements. There would be a meeting of spinning and swirling bodies. Dust and dirt was being thrown into the air as the two fought savagely.

Upon hearing and seeing the battle was in progress, Pete took the makeshift spear and approached the raging animals. Only then did he realize the closeness of the infighting prevented him from helping Amigo. Feeling quite helpless, Pete began to pray. He asked the Lord to intercede and in some way spare Amigo's life.

Again everything seemed like an eternity, but it had only been moments since the battle had begun. Suddenly out of the enraging battle Amigo emerged bleeding heavily from the right side of his head. His right ear looked to be shredded and torn, ripped by the razor sharp claws of the dangerous cougar. Although injured and slowed from the loss of blood, Amigo courageously continued his onslaught against the larger opponent.

Moving with amazing agility and evidently surprising the cat, Amigo charged and buried his teeth deep into one of the feline's upper legs. He shook his head violently with jaws locked in an ironclad grip. The mountain lion was just too big and strong, and spun and leaped into the air. The cat literally threw Amigo off and away.

Amigo was lying on the ground barely able to move. Due to the loss of blood and expended energy he appeared to be helpless.

The cougar was closing in for the kill when Pete jabbed its flank with the handmade spear. Intimidated and enraged by this new enemy, the cat focused all of its attention entirely on Pete. Pete continued to thrust the weapon fiercely at the cougar's flank. Now Pete had become endangered and he wished he had taken a little more time in creating the make-shift spear.

The defiant cat faced Pete as he continued to poke and thrust the spear at the lion's big frame. Repeatedly Pete jabbed the weapon to no avail. Now the cougar was on the offense. It raised its front paw and with lightning quick speed slapped the javelin from the grasp of Pete's hands. At the same time, the awesome power of the blow knocked Pete backwards and down to the ground. Pete prepared himself to meet the cat with his bare hands as that's all he had to defend himself with. In all the excitement the jack-knife had been left some twenty feet away.

Amigo, seeing Pete was in instant danger made a try to pull himself up, but as hard as he tried, it just wasn't possible. The huge lion eyed both fallen opponents as if it were trying to decide who to attack first. Then the cat slowly began moving towards Amigo.

Chapter 11

Kapow—kapow—kapow— rifle fire thundered through the canyon, then was faintly heard again and again and again as it echoed through the mountains. The bullets struck the earth thrusting dirt near the stalking mountain lion who was about to leap on its helpless foe.

Amigo lay still, covered about the head and shoulders by red stains of blood and fully at the mercy of the cat. The cougar evidently having heard gun shots before, whirled and with great swiftness bounded into the forest and disappeared.

Pete was still sitting on the ground trying to piece together the last few moments as he watched the big cat vanish into a thicket of dense brush and tall trees. Soon after, he heard a booming voice.

"Dag nab it, gol darn critter, how could ah miss that ol' catamount?"

Pete looked up and saw Jesse descending down a steep hill and mumbling minor obscenities to himself. In one hand Jesse was holding the 30-30 rifle and with the other he was motioning in the direction of the vanished mountain lion.

As Jesse closed in on Pete and Amigo, he stopped and shouted. "That onery ol' critter shore spent one of his nine lives this day. Gol darn lion was mitey lucky muh aim was off."

"Man alive Jesse, am I glad to see you, you got here just in time or Amigo and I would have become cat food." Pete pushed himself up and off the ground and walked in Jesse's direction with an outstretched hand. "What in blazes brought you out this way?"

"Ah'll tell ya 'bout it later, let's take a look at yore dawg an see whut's to be done."

Amigo had regained enough strength and was sitting up when Pete and Jesse reached him. The blood had stopped flowing and had started to clog up in his thick coat of hair.

"He looks a terrible mess, but I think he'll be okay." Pete was uncertain and he looked to Jesse for reassurance.

"All that darn blood makes it look wurse than it is. Don'tcha worree Pete. He'll be just as fine as frog hair in a day or two," Jesse echoed.

He knelt down beside Amigo and gave him a pat then continued, "Ya shore are a sight. Ah'll be darned if ah ever come across a dawg the likes of ya'll. Yes siree, yore some kind of dawg."

Pete nodded in agreement and added anxiously, "I've got some veterinary salve that I use on my hands for cuts and callouses. Let's get him back to camp so we can clean his wounds and apply some medicine."

With all the racket and excitement the young fawn had been completely forgotten. The mother was still standing where she had been all the while and she began to stomp. In repetition she would raise a front leg in the air and swiftly bring it down to the ground. This action brought immediate attention from Pete and Jesse.

Jesse exclaimed in surprise, "Well ah'll be. Whut in tarnation is that deer in such a stew about?"

"Oh boy," Pete declared. "Her little one is down in that hole and I forgot all about it. What with all the ruckus and such!" He threw his hands up in desperation. "We have to get that fawn out as quick as we can."

Pete looked around for the jack-knife and ropes and immediately ran to reclaim them. After retrieving these items, he returned to the excavation and the imprisoned fawn.

Amigo, although injured and in need of medical attention, looked on approvingly, he watched anxiously as Jesse lowered Pete into the hole and then rose to all fours as Jesse pulled the young deer up and out.

The mother called to her young one and the fawn promptly scooted to her side. She carefully looked over the fawn from head to toe and after deciding it was unharmed began to retreat into the forest.

Pete had pulled himself out of the hole just in time to join Jesse and Amigo watch the doe stop and look at them. It were as if she was saying thanks. Then she and her happy fawn bounded into the forest and they were gone from sight.

Chapter 12

Pete and Jesse didn't waste any time in getting Amigo back to camp.

Amigo had lost a good amount of blood. Pete immediately began to wash and cleanse the wounds. He was relieved to find that most of them were superficial. Only a wound on Amigo's right shoulder was deep and caused some serious concern. It turned out the ear looked much worse than it really was.

Pete came to the conclusion that he didn't have to take Amigo to a veterinarian, at least not at the present time. He decided he would keep a close watch on all the injuries and check often for any signs of digression. As long as there wasn't any sign of infection, Amigo should be fine in a few days.

Jesse, who had been assisting Pete was happy to see Amigo wasn't any worse off than he was. Now, he finally asked Pete about the deadly encounter with the catamount.

Pete related the story telling Jesse all that had happened from beginning to end.

"Jesse, my friend." Pete had taken hold of both of Jesse's shoulders giving him a gentle shake. "Amigo and I want to thank you. You certainly came along in the nick of time. I hate to think of what might have taken place. Thank you."

"Well it twarn't nothin'. Y'all would of done me the same. Ah couldn't find a trace of y'all, so ah reckoned somethin' was amiss. Ah started to mosey aroun' and when ah heard all the commotion a goin', ah run up over the hill yonder and saw the fix y'all were in. Ah'm shore glad ah was able to help."

Pete changed the subject and told Jesse that he was real sorry, but he and Amigo would be leaving Monday morning providing Amigo was up to the task.

He invited Jesse to stay for a farewell supper of homemade chili, crackers and cheese, and some hot black coffee. Jesse was pleased to accept the invitation.

The conversation during supper was mostly about where Pete and Amigo would be going next. There were assurances from both that they would see each other in the future.

Amigo couldn't have been feeling very good because he had left his dinner untouched but he readily drank from his water dish.

When supper was finished, Pete, Jesse and Amigo said their so-longs, but not goodbye, as it was re-affirmed they would meet again.

Pete watched Jesse saunter down the road and after a final wave of hands Pete turned to the waiting chores and began washing the dishes. It had been one hectic day and both he and Amigo were ready for a good night's sleep.

It was a cool and pleasant evening. Pete lay awake listening to a light breeze wend its way through the leaves of the riverside alders. Amigo was asleep and absolutely still. In the distance Pete could hear the mournful cries of coyotes echoing across and through the canyons. The eerie wails made Pete aware that this was their country. The wilderness didn't belong to man, it really was meant for all the animals that inhabited the mountains and deserts. Pete looked down at Amigo, closed his eyes and was soon fast asleep himself.

Saturday and Sunday proved to be the norm without any extra or adverse conditions coming into play. Amigo's wounds were healing nicely but Pete guessed it would be at least another week before the marks of the battle would disappear for good. Even so, Amigo was up to giving chase whenever he spied a pesky chipmunk or a speedy little ground squirrel. One thing for sure, his pursuits were at a much slower pace and he didn't expend the usual energy. He still was able to show the troublesome rodents that he was still the bull of the woods.

When he wasn't involved in watching the two-ring circus, Pete was down in the river tending his sluice. Color showed in the clean-up on both days but amounted to very little. Not a nugget was found. Pete quit at noon on Sunday and began to pack for the next leg of the journey.

Amigo was well aware that a ride in the pick-up was close at hand. He followed Pete wherever he went.

While Pete was writing a grocery list, Amigo would interrupt him by thrusting his nose repetitively into the tablet. This caused Pete to scribble over some of the legible words. Pete chuckled, "You're always up to something, aren't you? Well, we're not leaving until tomorrow. Why don't you just settle down."

Amigo answered by tilting his head from side to side. Tired of being ignored, he lay down under the truck and continued to watch Pete until he fell asleep.

That night Pete re-affirmed his decision to cross Oregon to the northeastern part of the state. He had never placered in the area. Since he had the standing invitation from his old friend, Lee Patterson, he would be foolish not to take his pal up on the offer. Pete and Lee had become good and lasting friends while serving in the U.S. Air Force during the Korean War.

Lee had written Pete during the winter extending the invitation. The letter included directions to his claim situated west of Baker City.

Pete was planning all along to visit Lee, but his plans were for sometime in mid-August. Weather and other circumstances had pushed his agenda ahead of schedule. It was only coming up on the last week of June.

Chapter 13

Pete and Amigo were up and moving at the crack of dawn. After several cups of black coffee and fire-toasted muffins, Pete finished loading the truck and they were off to Oregon.

They could complete the trip in 10 or 12 hours, but Pete wasn't in any hurry. He planned to camp overnight after 8 hours of steady driving. He would pick up supplies tomorrow and still arrive sometime shortly after mid-day.

Although it was Monday, traffic was still on the heavy side. Cars, trucks, motorhomes and an occasional motorcycle all sped by as Pete kept the old pick-up at 50 M.P.H.

The 8 hours seemed to have passed quickly. Pete started to look for a road leading off the highway and a likely spot to camp. Soon, he came across a National Forest access road and followed it until he found a suitable site. The setting was a pretty mountain brook surrounded by towering pine trees.

Amigo shot out of the pick-up like a bullet and promptly began to check out the entire area. Every bush, tree and rock was thoroughly inspected. If deemed so, it was quickly marked. He was proclaiming the territory his turf and was alerting all the critters, large and small to take notice. Of course, he himself was not aware that he would soon be leaving. It wouldn't have mattered anyway. It wasn't very long before he spied a pert little chipmunk sitting on a stump and the chase was on. Once more the little rodent was victorious as Amigo lost by a hair. The chipmunk had scampered into a hole at the base of a nearby tree and disappeared. Amigo was perplexed as usual and wouldn't give up. He continued to circle the tree looking for the hidden quarry. This was a scene Pete had witnessed time and time again, and it still tickled him as it always brought on a smile. Amigo's face formed a quizzical expression as he sniffed and snuffed at the hole the speedy rodent had fled into.

The night brought a cool steady drizzle that lasted until daybreak. As the sun slowly rose up over the mountains the shimmering drops of rain sputtered to a halt. Within the hour Pete and Amigo were on their way again.

At 10:30 A.M. they reached the pleasant town of John Day. Pete figured that this would be the best place to buy the needed provisions. Upon entering the parking lot of a local supermarket Pete noticed a hardware store was also available.

Pete stroked Amigo and told him he would return in a short time. He started towards the hardware store, checking his list as he walked along. Number one and most important were batteries for the portable radio. This was Pete's only contact with news, sports and weather, and sole source of entertainment.

When the shopping list was all accounted for, the pair shared an ice cream cone and continued on their way. They were less than two hours from Lee's camp.

Chapter 14

Pete left the highway turning onto a gravel road and proceeded northward following Lee's written directions. As he slowed down, the truck with pebbles and stones plinking the under-carriage alerted Amigo to the new surroundings. Pete knew he had to cross a small ravine then a second cattle guard before he turned onto the trail. This road led down into a deep canyon and Lee's claim. The trail was close to nine miles from the highway and because of the poor traveling conditions it took them a long time. As they slowly descended down the steep grade Pete kept pumping the brake. This was the only way he could keep the pick-up under control. After numerous switchbacks and one last long steep grade Pete was happy to see Lee's silver Airstream shimmering amongst the trees.

The location and setting was just as Lee had described it, but he had forgotten to say how beautiful it really was. On the nearside and flowing south, the creek followed alongside a magnificent meadow. The meadow was covered with thousands of pink, purple, white and yellow wild flowers. Looking across the meadow and on the far side of the swift water, hundreds upon hundreds of thick pine and fir concealed the mountainside.

This stretched as far as the eye could see. North and on both sides of the stream, the rim of the forest rose and fell in splendor. If a person looked carefully and directly across the creek you could see a tunnel. The entrance had been boarded up for safety reason. Tailing piles were seen alongside the excavation down to the creek. This had to be the hard rock mine that was in operation around the turn of the century. Nature was doing a fine job of erasing the only scar left on the mountain.

Pete pulled up and parked beside the Airstream. Lee's Ford Bronco was parked nearby but nobody appeared to be anywhere in sight.

Pete and Amigo hopped out of the pick-up and Amigo began to explore the new location. Out of the pick-up with the engine turned off, Pete could hear the unmistakable whine of a small motor.

"That's Lee dredging, Amigo. C'mon fella, let's go find the ol' coot. I'll bet he will be surprised to see us."

Pete listened until he was positive where the steady hum of the small engine was coming from.

He and Amigo started to walk upstream. "C'mon boy, let's go."

It wasn't long before the pair were met by a playful yellow Labrador pup. Pete estimated the dog to be somewhere around six months old. He attempted to grab Amigo by his collar, but Amigo was too fast and was rapidly approaching the young pup.

The two animals stood side by side giving each other the once over as Pete drew a deep breath and spoke softly, "Easy Amigo, easy fella. Be a good dog. Don't you hurt that pup. Easy boy."

Evidently the encounter with the fawn and the cougar had matured Amigo and within a few moments the two dogs were off and running.

A sigh of relief came over Pete and he had a smile on his face as he spied Lee's dredge.

Lee, wearing a wet suit, was submerged under water. He was busy applying the nozzle into the bottom of the rock and gravel laden stream. The average depth of the creek ran some two feet or so. Pete could see that Lee had dredged out at least an eight foot hole.

Pete decided to have a little fun with the situation. Since Lee was not aware of his newly arrived visitors, Pete quietly slipped into the creek and shut down the engine. Quick as a blink of an eye Pete was out of the water hiding behind a large pine.

Just as Pete had hoped, Lee surfaced clearing his mask, and grumbled a few choice words about the idle engine. Lee gave one strong pull on the rope and started the motor then resumed the dredging.

Pete laughed, then went through the same motions again and hid behind the pine.

This time, Lee was a little more deliberate and voiced some well chosen words towards his silent engine. With a frown showing, he yanked the starter rope successfully and slid down under the water.

Pete waited a little longer this time. He wanted to be absolutely sure Lee was caught up in his work before he repeated the sequence once more.

Lee approaching the dredge, mask in hand looked like he was fit to be tied. "What in blue blazes is going on?" He threw his hands up in desperation. "This is downright ridiculous." Then while appearing like he was on the verge of pulling his hair out by the roots, he heard a strange voice.

Pete stepped out from behind the pine wearing a broad grin on his face and joked. "Are you having a hard time, my friend?"

Lee was taken by complete surprise. He realized what had taken place and he began to laugh. "Why you old son-of-a-gun, you had me fit to be tied. How are you Pete?"

Both men were laughing as they met and shook hands.

"I couldn't resist, Lee, I haven't had that much fun in a long time. I really laid one on you."

"Well, I'll tell you, Pete, I was ready to give that machine a good swift kick. I owe you one, pardner."

"Okay, I reckon I've got it coming." Pete admitted.

Meanwhile the two dogs who had momentarily been forgotten by their owners had returned from their play and were panting heavily. Both dogs jumped in the stream and lay down to drink some water and cool off at the same time.

"It sure looks like those two have had quite a run. They're plumb wore out. What do you call your dog, Pete?" Then Lee added as an afterthought, "That one's name is Toby."

"That's Amigo." Pete answered proudly.

Upon hearing his name Amigo left the creek with Toby following close behind. Both animals sidled up alongside Pete and began to shake themselves vigorously, showering Pete with water.

Again Lee was laughing. "Good boys.... good dogs. That will teach him. Come on Pete, let's get something nice and cold to drink ourselves."

After ridding himself of the wetsuit and wearing more appropriate clothing, Lee brought out a pitcher of ice cold lemonade. There was a table and chairs under a large fir that offered some nice shade as it was unseasonably hot for June.

Lee nodded his head and asked, "Tell me, where have you two been and what have you been doing?"

Pete related the whole story to Lee, beginning with his acquisition of Amigo. The how, when, where and why. He told of the meeting with Jesse and his "boys." Lastly he told Lee of the perilous encounter with the mountain lion.

Lee in return brought Pete up to date including some good news about the claim. Color was plentiful. He was finding plenty of nuggets. Many were a pennyweight to three pennyweight with the largest a little over a half an ounce.

Amigo and Toby kept themselves busy chasing chipmunks and ground squirrels. When they couldn't find any to bother, they chased each other.

Lee and Pete spent the remainder of the afternoon setting up Pete's camp.

Lee was a few years older than Pete but in good physical shape having spent the last nine years mining. He had been fortunate enough to receive an early retirement with a good pension and full benefits.

Lee was stocky and solid with wide shoulders that gave him a powerful appearance. His hair was dark brown, worn crew cut style with no sign of greying. He was a pleasant man with a good sense of humor.

Lee put together a fine supper consisting of biscuits and gravy, fried eggs, sausage and black coffee. To Lee's delight, Pete offered that the meal was the best he had ever eaten.

"Your exaggerating, aren't you, Pete?"

"Well, darn sure one of the best." Pete answered.

The two old friends washed dishes and cleaned up the pots and pans. Then Lee brewed another pot of coffee while Pete built a campfire. They sat around the campfire and talked for hours while drinking plenty of coffee.

Amigo and Toby, tired from the day's many chases lay nearby.

Pete and Lee finally decided to turn in and call it a day.

Chapter 15

The next day on Lee's advice Pete chose a likely spot to begin mining. Upon walking a short distance downstream from camp, the two men came across an excellent place to hi-bank. The banks rose at least ten feet above the water level of the creek.

Pointing his finger toward the chosen placer, Lee quipped, "That should keep you busy for quite a while."

Pete nodded his agreement.

Within the hour Pete was hard at work swinging the pick into the rock and gravel laden bank. He was able to shovel the loose and broken rock directly into the sluicebox.

Pete worked a long and hard six hours that first day. He was rewarded nicely with several nuggets, one weighing two pennyweight. He also panned out some flake and flour. This is how it went day after day, Pete working the placer and being handsomely compensated for his daily efforts.

Most evenings were spent by warm glowing campfires and drinking many cups of hot black coffee. The two friends told and retold stories from the past and into the present.

Amigo and Toby completely occupied each day roughhousing, chasing and cavorting until they exhausted themselves.

The month of July passed quickly. Everything was doing fine until a sudden and turbulent storm struck one early August evening.

Lee and Pete were enjoying their usual campfire chat when they heard a loud roar rumble through the canyon. The eerie streaks of lightning flickered through the tree tops. Then a strong wind came roaring through the canyon snapping limbs like matchsticks. A deluge of thunder and lightning mixed with periods of hail and heavy rain engulfed the tree within moments.

The pair with Amigo and Toby at their heels scurried as fast as possible seeking safety in their respective shelters.

The storm had come and gone fast and furiously. In less than an hour the stars had reappeared in a clear nighttime sky but one couldn't help but notice the unmistakable odor of sulphur lingering in the air.

Little did Pete and Lee know but in two weeks time they would be going their separate ways.

A few days after the violent storm, Lee observed smoke to the north and west of the claim. He called the gray haze to Pete's attention. "Smoke is rising over those tree tops northwest of here, Pete. That could cause some problems if its what I think it is."

"I sure hope your wrong," Pete gasped.

The two men decided they would keep a close watch on the smoke-filled sky but they would continue their mining operations.

Since they were concerned, both Lee and Pete were not surprised when two days later they had a visitor.

A U.S. Forest Service representative stopped by and advised the two men that they would be required to evacuate the area as soon as possible. Preferably today but certainly no later than tomorrow.

The man told them that the recent storm had started the fire. The fire had already burned 9000 square acres. He also told the two men that there was a good chance that the flames could reach Lee's claim by the next evening.

The rest of the day Pete helped Lee dismantle the dredge and load the Bronco. In return Lee helped Pete to pack up and load.

When they were finished the two friends made a joint decision to wait until early morning to leave. Darkness had set in and both men were ready for a good nights sleep.

That night Pete reflected that Labor Day was only a couple of weeks away and he and Amigo would have had to leave Lee and Toby regardlessly. He had been planning to work his own claim in Idaho before heading south into Arizona.

The early snows were not really that far off and the white powdery stuff could arrive as soon as mid-September. There would be plenty of warm days through September and October but one would be wise to keep an eye on the weather.

Early the next morning after a hardy breakfast Pete and Lee said their goodbyes.

Pete and Amigo had a two-day trip into east central Idaho. Again they would camp along the way.

Chapter 16

On the second day after their departure from Oregon, the nomadic twosome reached their destination some forty miles north-northwest of Challis, Idaho.

Pete readily chose a campsite on a gravel bench overlooking a pristine stream a few feet below. The view was breathtaking and Pete stood in awe of the beauty surrounding him. He noticed the sheltered bend on the mountain slope, almost, but not quite hiding the mouth of a silent running brook. The brook discharged its waters into the main and larger stream.

Pete spoke to Amigo, "This is our claim, Amigo. What do you think of it?"

Amigo seemed to have understood and as if he was telling Pete he was happy with his new location, he ran down to the stream and had a drink of water.

It was almost noon when Pete had finished setting up the camp and he was quite hungry. As usual, Amigo was making his routine inspections over the camping area.

After a hastily prepared lunch of sandwiches, cookies and some coffee, Pete sought out his gold pan.

Pete had purchased the claim the preceding fall. Since the site appeared to be fairly free of any recent placering, Pete thought it would be a good idea to scout around. He started to look for the most likely spots along the stream. First he searched the area around the mouth of the small brook. Then using his experience, it was just as he had suspected, color began showing almost at once. Nothing to brag about, but color, mostly flakes, nothing larger, but he really didn't expect much in the overburden.

Digging down to bedrock might produce a whole different outcome. Pete decided that this was a good place to start. He would start in earnest the next morning. First he and Amigo had some exploring to do.

Amigo had returned to camp and was sleeping peacefully on a soft bed of pine needles. Through time the needles had fallen from the thick stand of pines and covered the entire camping area.

Amigo rose quickly as Pete sauntered into camp. He sensed a forthcoming walk and he playfully jumped on his master.

Since they had driven in from the upstream end, Pete thought it would be a good idea to have a look downstream. He wanted to familiarize himself with the entire location.

Amigo led the way taking time to smell and mark whatever he pleased. Every once in a while a pesky rodent would capture his attention and he would give harmless chase. When Pete thought they had gone far enough, probably close to a mile, he and Amigo walked away from the creek and proceeded back to camp by way of the main road.

On the return trip to camp Pete was surprised to find a recently abandoned campsite where the creek was separated from the road. He surmised the campsite was only a short distance, a little more than a quarter of a mile from his own camp. Unlike his campsite that was hidden from view by the stand of trees, this camping area was easily accessible to anyone.

By the time the wandering pair reached camp, Pete had tired some, so it was a quick and easy supper similar to lunch.

After cleaning up and one last cup of coffee, he and Amigo turned in for the night.

The next three weeks were pretty routine and passed by amazingly fast.

Then one early mid-September morning the cool and crisp mountain air caused Pete to shake and shiver when he left his comfortable camper. He started the campfire as quickly as possible to ward off the morning chill. Soon he had downed his first cup of coffee relishing the warmth the hot drink provided. Finally the sun began to rise up over the mountain and the air became warm and pleasant. Pete whispered, "This is going to be a mighty fine day."

If he could have only foreseen the coming events, he would have broken camp and he and Amigo would have hightailed out of there quicker than a blink of an eye.

Of course there always would be moments of fun and laughter. The hilarious antics that Amigo and his rodent friends always managed to stir up, created plenty of playful trouble.

One such event happened before a week had passed. On this particular day Pete had spent more time than normal working the diggings. He was quite tired and his muscles were aching. He decided to lie down in the back of the pick-up and take an afternoon nap. The sun was nice and warm and Pete was asleep in minutes. He had slept but a short time when he was startled and awakened from his afternoon siesta.

Amigo was making enough noise to raise the dead. He was barking and growling as vociferous as Pete had ever heard. Alarmed, Pete looked out of the side window to see what was causing all the commotion. At first he was concerned but as he watched the proceedings he became amused and started to laugh.

Less than fifty feet away was a creature to behold. It was a magnificent moose, a cow. It was the most majestic animal he had ever laid eyes on.

She was standing perfectly still, unafraid with her head looking over her shoulder, staring at the loud, noisy and arrogant meddler.

Amigo was beside himself, but yet wary enough not to close the distance between the two. It was a Mexican standoff.

The cow moose stood defiant, silent and unyielding. Her eyes were fixed on the strange and noisy animal that was making a fool of itself. On the other hand, Amigo was chastising the large creature and claiming his territory.

Amigo still growling sensed that the moose was more than he could handle, but he refused to move in any direction.

The ruckus came to an end when Pete, unknowingly climbing out of the truck, alerted the moose to uneven odds and possible danger. She immediately ran off into the forest and disappeared.

Amigo, walking proud and tall approached Pete preparing for the praise he knew he would receive.

Chapter 17

We have all heard the quote.... "When it rains it pours."
Well Pete didn't know but a whole lot of moisture was about
to fall, and in frequent fashion.

A few days after the confrontation with the cow moose,
Pete realized that he had to keep close tabs on Amigo,
especially when he was busy at the diggin's. He and Amigo
had bonded so closely that it would have broken Pete's heart
to lose the canine. Pete chose to keep Amigo on a chain and
under restraint.

Well the next encounter proved the restraining action was
a good decision and Pete was glad he had used the good
judgement.

Only two days had passed and Pete was at the placer.
Amigo was attached to a chain up on the gravel bench. The
chain was fastened to a sturdy alder some seventy feet away.

Once again Pete was alerted to some kind of disturbance,
this time there wasn't any barking but Amigo was growling
and he was serious. Pete could see Amigo clearly and the hair
on his neck and shoulders was standing straight up. Since the
cougar incident, Pete always kept his .38 Smith and Wesson
handy. He dropped the shovel, picked up the weapon and ran
to Amigo's side.

Whatever Amigo was growling at was in the brush and out of sight somewhere off to the left. While scanning the area, Pete delivered a few pats to Amigo's head.

Several minutes later after a thorough inspection, Pete decided whatever had upset Amigo was now gone and any possible danger had passed. Pete assured Amigo that everything was all right and he returned to his work.

He had been back a short time and again Amigo began to growl and the same thing happened all over again. This time, however, Pete became aware of the reason and nature of the disturbance.

A short distance away but in plain view was a six or seven month old black bear cub. Pete could only estimate the age of the cub. The bear probably had been born the preceding winter. The young black bear was curious but cautious as it watched Pete and Amigo. Pete suddenly caught another movement directly behind the cub and this created a much different predicament.

Appearing out of the brush and standing on its haunches was another black bear. This bear was much larger and Pete was sure the bear was the young one's mother. Pete exhaled, his voice cracked and he instantly reached down to Amigo. "Easy boy, easy, you just take it easy."

The mother bear appeared to be in a bad mood and plainly disturbed by the present situation, but she was also wary of the trespassers. She remained still, her mouth open but silent, and her paws were held high in the air. The bear sent shivers down Pete's spine and he came to a quick conclusion. He and Amigo had more trouble than they bargained for.

Pete knew instantly that the .38 was useless unless it was fired as a scare tactic to frighten the bears away.

Amigo continued to growl intermittently but had quit pulling on the chain. Pete still kept a firm grip on his collar.

Pete didn't know whether they should run, stand still or fire the weapon. The situation was not at all to Pete's liking and certainly favored the bears. Pete guessed the mother bear's weight to be close to 330 pounds. Whatever the poundage, more than enough adversity for he and Amigo.

Just at that moment Pete heard the sound of an engine whining as if it were drawing a heavy load. Whether it was a car or truck he didn't know but the irritating noise caught the mother bears attention. She momentarily dropped to all fours and focused on the new and noisy intrusion.

Pete used these few seconds wisely. He quickly unchained Amigo and he and the dog walked quietly down to the stream and back to camp. The bears had not followed and Pete surmised the vehicle had caused enough confusion to let them escape unharmed.

Pete relaxed after a few watchful moments, then wiped his brow with his handkerchief and exclaimed, "Wow, that was too close, boy." He continued to address Amigo. "Well big fella, we've seen it all, huh? First the skunk, then Jesse's boys, the cougar and the moose, and last I hope these darn bothersome bears. That sure don't leave many more, does it? We're running out of critters, Amigo."

Chapter 18

September had come and gone and from time to time a slight dusting of snow covered the ground. The soft white flakes soon melted away as the warm sun reached the earth.

Pete guessed they could endure another month without too much hardship due to the weather. He did expect cool and cold mornings, evenings and nights and snowfalls of some depth but nothing too serious. He decided to pay close attention to the daily weather reports. Pete knew it was too soon to leave for Arizona. The temperatures there would still be reaching into triple digits.

On the first Sunday in October, Pete and Amigo awakened to the first snow of any consequence. The snow had fallen during the night and had laid a smooth blanket of powder some three to four inches in depth.

Pete was busy starting the campfire while Amigo frolicked in the cold and fluffy softness. Amigo had not paid any attention to the small amounts that had fallen earlier but this was lots of fun. He would bury his nose into the snow, then suddenly throw his head up and leap into the air. The morning air was brisk but the sun was bright and the freshly fallen snow would be gone by early afternoon.

After a couple of cups of hot black coffee Pete joined Amigo in play. It wasn't long before he had tired, and he went back to the task of making breakfast.

There wasn't any apparent reason, but Amigo broke off his romp in the snow and ran quickly towards the main road. Pete called out to him without any success and watched Amigo disappear from sight. It wasn't like Amigo to disregard Pete's commands. Pete removed the frying bacon from the fire and went in hot pursuit of Amigo. When Pete reached the road he glanced in the direction he had last seen Amigo run. He was surprised, to say the least, and Pete began jogging towards the scene shaking his head in wonderment.

A few hundred yards down the road, a lady was sitting smack dab right in the middle of the trail rubbing her lower leg. Amigo was showering the woman with affection and as Pete closed the distance he could see Amigo licking the lady's forehead.

Pete heard the lady whisper, "Oh thank you, thank you. You're a good dog, a pretty dog, thank you."

Pete had reached the two and after introducing himself asked, "Are you all right, are you hurt?"

Pete offered his hand to help the lady to her feet, but the lady rejected, exclaiming, "Please let me sit awhile. I'm all right, but I think I may have sprained my ankle. At first your friend here, gave me a scare but I soon realized he came to help. Oh my gosh, I'm sorry, my name is Nancy, Nancy Healy."

After a few minutes of rest, Nancy asked Pete to help her to her feet. Pete readily obliged and as he was assisting her, Nancy told him how she happened to be in the aggravating situation. Nancy explained that she, her husband and her son were camped a little ways down the road. They had been here for a few days and her husband and son were avid fishermen. While they were out chasing trout, she had chosen to jog down the road and enjoy the beauty the snow had added to the mountains. It was her misfortune to stub her foot in a tire rut on the trail. This caused her to twist her ankle and fall to the ground striking her head on the hard gravel road. Nancy pointed to her head that become somewhat swollen and was snowing signs of contusions. Nancy expressed that she had momentarily blacked out and when she had shaken the cob-webs from her head, there was this beautiful dog. The dog had snuggled up against her and he was licking the bruised area of her forehead. Pete arrived and knew the rest.

Pete asked, "Are you sure you're okay, can I help you back to your camp?"

"That would be nice, yes, thank you." Nancy answered.

Pete asked Nancy to wait with Amigo while he went to get the pick-up.

In a matter of minutes, Pete returned with the truck and helped Nancy get inside. Amigo hopped into the back and they were on their way to the Healy camp. The campsite turned out to be the one Pete and Amigo had come across before. As they drove up next to a travel trailer, a man and teenaged boy had come out and were hurrying towards the pick-up.

Nancy introduced Pete and Amigo to her husband Bill, and her son, Tim. Then she had to re-tell the whole story all over again. Upon completion, Pete and Amigo were invited to stay for coffee and sweet rolls.

Pete readily accepted the invitation. It was nice having folks to visit. Amigo was treated like royalty and he was rewarded with a delicious donut.

Pete learned the Healy family was from Boise. After a lot of conversation he also learned that the Healy's were respon-sible for scaring off the bears.

Pete told that story to the family and credited them with saving him and Amigo from serious harm.

After a short but pleasant visit Pete found out that the family would be leaving for home. Pete and Amigo returned to camp. They had made some new friends and had a standing invitation to call on the Healy's any time they cared to.

Chapter 19

Indian summer had set in and after the initial snowfall the next two weeks of October were warm and pleasant. Pete had been finding a good amount of color including some real nice nuggets and with all things considered, doing quite well. A couple more weeks in the diggings then he and Amigo would start south.

After spending four to five hours a day confined to the chain, Amigo was always excited and ready to romp when Pete quit work and turned him loose. There were always the pesky rodents to chase and occupy his time.

After all the altercations with the other animals, ironic as it was, this was the day Amigo would require medical attention. Pete would have to seek out a veterinarian.

On this eventful evening Pete was busy fixing dinner and Amigo was running all over the area. Upon not seeing Amigo for quite sometime, Pete became concerned. He called him a number of times and failed to get a response. He decided that he had better look for him.

About fifteen minutes later after calling him many times, Pete saw Amigo coming towards him. Amigo's tongue was darting in and out of his mouth. He was shaking his head vigorously and lifting his front paw, sliding it alongside his snout and stopping often to do so. When the two met each other, Pete saw that Amigo's nose and jaws looked like a pin cushion. It was covered with porcupine quills.

They returned to camp immediately and Pete tried to extract the quills, but he was unsuccessful. He had only managed to eliminate four quills and he believed he was causing more pain to Amigo then necessary.

The nearest and largest town was Salmon. It was over an hour's drive, mostly downgrade, with many switchbacks and curves but Pete didn't have a choice. He was sure the veterinarian clinic would be closed but he had to try and find some help. He felt helpless and was really concerned about the pain he knew Amigo to be in.

After a very slow but safe trip down the mountain Pete arrived in Salmon at 7 P.M. He stopped at the very first service station he came to and asked for directions to the nearest veterinarian services.

The man at the service station gave Pete directions to the only two veterinarians in town. The first, a clinic less than four blocks away and the second, a little more than a mile away on the north end of town. The man also offered information that the veterinarian farthest away had his office adjacent to his home and that would be Pete's best bet.

Pete thanked him and took his advice and drove to the north end. Pete didn't have any trouble finding the place and saw the sign as he drove into the driveway.

L.M. Kethler
D.V.M.

He left Amigo in the pick-up and started for the front door. The door opened as Pete was about to knock.

A kindly looking man with gray hair and a pleasant smile on his face looked at Pete with some surprise and said. "Yes, can I help you?"

Pete answered quickly, concern showing upon his face. "My dog is in my truck and I'm afraid he's in a lot of pain." Pete added immediately, "He got into trouble with a porcupine and he sure came out on the short end of the stick."

The veterinarian looked over his shoulder into the house and spoke softly, "I'll be busy for a little while. You don't mind do you?"

Pete didn't hear any answer if there was one.

The doctor motioned with his hand and spoke simultaneously. "Bring your dog around to my office door and I'll meet you there." The veterinarian added, "My wife and I were just about to go out to dinner but this won't take very long if you help me."

Doctor Kethler opened the office door allowing Pete and Amigo to enter and explained. "Since my assistant isn't here, I'll have to ask you to hold him while I administer the anesthetic."

Doctor Kethler noted that Amigo was a handsome animal and asked if Pete wanted to leave him overnight.

Pete told him that he really would like to take him back to camp.

The veterinarian nodded knowingly. "Help me get him up on that table and we'll get started."

After Amigo received the anesthetic, he was asleep in moments. Fifteen minutes later Doctor Kethler had extracted thirty-three porcupine quills from the muzzle area. Then, he and Pete carried the sleeping canine out to the pick-up. Using care, they placed him comfortably on the front seat.

Pete returned with the doctor to the office. He took out his wallet to make payment and said, "How much do I owe you, Doctor?"

Dr. Kethler motioned his hand towards Pete and said "You do something nice for someone the next time you get a chance."

Pete asked, "Are you sure? I really appreciate this."

"I know that," Dr. Kethler replied and went on, "I can see how much your dog means to you. Just do as I ask. Do something nice when you get an opportunity to do so."

Pete promised he would do as the doctor asked, then gratefully added, "Thank you, doctor." He grasped Dr. Kethler's hand and said good-bye and thanked him once again.

Amigo was out like a light on the way back to camp. Every once in a while he would emit a strange and frightening sound. This worried Pete, but the doctor had told him to expect Amigo to be out of sorts for at least a day.

The next morning Pete had to awaken Amigo and help him out of the truck. Amigo had trouble standing and when he finally steadied he had a problem walking. He wobbled and weaved like a drunken sailor. By the end of the day Amigo was more like himself and Pete was greatly relieved.

Chapter 20

More than a week had passed and there hadn't been any more unfortunate incidents. Amigo had fully recovered and didn't appear to have suffered any after effects. Pete continued to work the placer and reap the rewards of his daily labor. The weather was holding and continued to stay on the mild side. Snow fell infrequently, mostly at night and melted away under the noon day sun. Another week and they would be on their way to Arizona. Pete would welcome the change of climate but he wasn't so sure of Amigo. Due to the cool and cold mornings Pete had shortened and moved his work schedule to later in the day. Now much of the day was spent gathering firewood, watching Amigo at play and anything else that was deemed necessary.

Even though it was many miles out of the way, Pete was giving serious thought about driving into Salmon when they left for Arizona. His thoughts were of Dr. Kethler's kindness and he thought it would be nice to thank him once again. The forest service road to Challis was more sensible and practical than the road down to Salmon. The numerous downgrades were not as steep and the Challis road was free of the troublesome switchbacks. Pete decided he would think on it.

Only three days before Pete and Amigo were due to leave, on the morning of October 28th, their destiny was decided for them. The morning appeared to be like any other autumn morning but this one soon proved to be much different.

At first Pete hadn't noticed anything strange or out of the ordinary. After building the campfire and drinking some black coffee, Pete became more aware of the immediate surroundings. For one thing he realized Amigo was lying quietly by the fire. Usually by this time, Amigo would be busy trying to rustle up a varmint.

Then he noticed the stillness on the mountain was downright quiet, so quiet, one could actually hear the silence. There wasn't a breeze in the air. Strangely the birds were not singing or chirping as usual. Pete scanned the camp-site trying to locate some movement. There wasn't any to be found. He finally focused on the only sound to be heard. That was the rippling of the water flowing steadily down the stream. Pete had become so used to this constant babble that he really hadn't heard it until now. An overwhelming and eerie feeling came over him.

Pete sat down and poured himself another cup of coffee. He spoke to Amigo. "Something's funny, fella. I don't know what's going on, but something's not right. Come here, boy. Come here."

Amigo rose and came to Pete and sat down beside him. Pete thought that he was just imagining things and began to nervously pat his companion. Amigo leaned against Pete's knee and accepted the affection.

Pete spoke again, "I guess I'm making a mountain out of a mole hill. I don't know. I've got this funny feeling. Maybe we should pack up and leave. What do you say, Amigo."

Amigo just sat still and looked up at Pete.

"Okay, I'm probably over reacting. I'm a might spooky. I reckon I'll have some breakfast." Pete was getting ready to peel some potatoes when he thought he had heard something, a faint noise, something like far off thunder. He listened carefully for a few moments. He still didn't know what it was. All of a sudden there was a loud roaring noise and Amigo jumped up from his sitting position. Pete looked at Amigo as he finally understood the cause of all his anxiety.

The mountain began to shake and rumble, causing numerous tremors to pass along and across the earth. Pete was visibly shaken and he whispered, "Earthquake."

Amigo also sensing danger, leaned hard against his master.

Pete's attention focused on the tremendous clamor surrounding him. Stones, rolling rock and huge boulders rained down the mountainside, smashing into trees and brush.

Suddenly, something of terrific force struck him high on his shoulder knocking him down to the ground. Pete felt overwhelming dizziness, everything surrounding him appeared to be spinning and swirling. Soon he lost control and succumbed to complete blackness.

When Pete awakened he could feel Amigo lying down beside him. "Amigo, how are you boy?"

Amigo assured Pete that he was all right by gently licking his master's forehead.

Pete was relieved for the moment. He smiled, then winced in pain as he felt as if a knife had pierced his shoulder blade. He began to rub his neck and shoulder area to make sure to his satisfaction that nothing had been broken. The shock of the tremendous blow he had received had slowed his senses and Pete was stunned as he realized for the first time, something else had taken place. He couldn't see.

He remained on the ground trying to gather his thoughts and above all remain calm. The loss of his sight was another and much more serious situation. Pete turned his head in all directions attempting to see. He was hoping for the best, but he was sadly disappointed. He began to blink his eye, slowly at first, then gradually at a more rapid pace and finally he could see something. He felt his hopes rising. He strained his eye trying harder to recognize his surroundings. Finally he could make out gray shapes, outlines, something like shadows.

Pete smiled and called out to Amigo. He watched as a faint gray shape approached. "Good dog, good boy."

Searching and scanning the campsite, he could just barely identify the larger objects. He recognized a tree, a boulder, then he saw the pick-up. Everything was gray and barely visible but at least he had some limited sight.

Pete immediately thought of the C.B. radio in the pickup truck. He had purchased the radio in case of an emergency and right now he was in dire need of help. He hoped he could reach someone, anyone to help him out of this dangerous position.

He rose from the ground and took a good hold of Amigo's collar and they walked slowly towards the truck. Pete was aware that it was impossible to drive the vehicle out, but he still checked the truck for any possible damage.

To his surprise Pete found the pick-up to be completely unharmed. He got in and started the engine. Then, turning on the C.B., he began to search the channels in hope of reaching some kind of help. He knew the chance of success was remote but he had to give it a try.

Over and over Pete scanned all forty channels. After failing to find any assistance, he finally gave up.

Pete was unsure of how long he had lain unconscious, but he was sure it was still early morning. The air was crisp and cool indicating this to be true. Pete was aware of the possible permanent loss of his eyesight. He also knew that time was of extreme importance. Again he called Amigo to his side.

Then with his partner leading, he walked to the rear of the truck.

Pete did his best to remain calm and began to gather items needed for a long walk out.

Chapter 21

Due to his present condition, Pete knew it would take much more time than usual to walk the 25 miles out to the highway. He could only hope and pray that he and Amigo would find assistance sooner.

Upon finding a few plastic grocery bags, Pete began stuffing one with extra clothing, a sweatshirt, a sweater and a goosedown vest. In another he placed a warm heavy blanket. If he had to spend the night on the mountain, he was going to be prepared. In the third and last sack Pete collected some snacks consisting of candy, cookies and a few apples. Not forgetting Amigo, he added a generous supply of dog biscuits and treats.

Pete sighed. "Well fella, I guess were ready to go." Then as an afterthought added, "Wait a minute boy, hold on."

With his limited vision Pete still decided to strap on the .38 revolver. The weapon could still come in mighty handy. While doing this, Pete ran his belt through the handles of the grocery bags allowing him the freedom and use of both hands.

Ready to go, Pete placed his walking stick in one hand and with the other he secured the leash to Amigo's collar. The lonely pair started out on their dangerous trip.

The forest service road ran parallel with the stream almost down to the highway. Most of the time Pete would be able to hear the waters of the meandering stream. This had to offer some well needed assistance.

Amigo led the way. He walked slowly and deliberately as if he knew Pete depended entirely upon him. He did a good job. He evaded the obstacles lying in the road. Rocks, boulders and tree limbs lay strewn on the road. Once in a while they would come upon an uprooted tree and have to detour into the brush in order to move on. Many times Pete tripped over a rock or a tree branch causing him to almost fall to the ground. Luckily he never completely lost his balance and managed to continue following Amigo at a very slow pace.

It seemed like forever, but in reality they had only been on their lonely walk a couple of hours when Pete decided to rest and have a bite to eat. Only then did he realize he had forgotten to bring something to drink. He stroked Amigo and quipped, "Oh well, I guess we both will be drinking out of the creek." After a short rest the two were soon on their way.

The day seemed to be extra long and Pete could only guess at their progress. At best he figured they could only cover a mile per hour, and that didn't include time spent in rest. Contemplating the situation, Pete realized that if they walked through the night, and he doubted this a reality, they still wouldn't reach the highway until the next evening.

Night time arrived and although Amigo walked with great care not to cause any further problems, Pete had to shorten his steps to more of a shuffle. He decided they would continue as long as possible.

Luckily, the harvest moon was shining brightly and did offer limited assistance and visibility. On the down side it also turned the night air extremely cold and this chilled Pete down to the bone.

Sometime later upon finding an uprooted tree lying across the road, Pete decided to stop and sleep for a while. Gathering as many pine boughs as possible he placed them on the leeward side of the big tree. He donned his extra clothing and lay down on the makeshift bed and covered himself with the blanket.

Amigo snuggled up close to Pete's side and soon the pair were sound asleep.

A few hours later Pete was awakened by the mournful cries of wailing coyotes seemingly closer than they actually were. Since he was awake he figured they might as well resume their trek.

As they moved slowly down the road, Pete estimated they had covered some nine or ten miles at most. He flinched and muttered, "Probably another fifteen miles to go." They continued through the chilling darkness.

A few hours after Pete and Amigo left their makeshift camp, daylight began to break on the horizon. Pete was sadly disappointed to find his eyesight had not gotten any better. Everything in view was either in shadow or completely indistinguishable.

As they walked further down the road, Pete suddenly became aware that they hadn't come across any obstructions for quite sometime.

Minutes later Pete thought he heard a faint humming noise in the far distance. He and Amigo stopped to listen. He hoped the sound he heard was not just his imagination. Upon hearing the sound again, a smile broke on his face as the humming noise turned into a steady roar.

"A truck, Amigo, I think I hear a logging truck."

Chapter 22

Surprised to find the lonely pair standing in the middle of the road, the driver of the truck brought the vehicle to a safe and abrupt stop. The man then withdrew from the idle truck and walked towards Pete and Amigo.

"Howdy, are you okay?" He added, "My name is Sam Roberts."

"Hi, am I glad to see you. I'm Pete, Pete Mitchell, and this is my pard, Amigo."

Time being of the utmost importance, Pete quickly told Sam of his urgent and serious plight.

Realizing Pete was indeed in a precarious situation, Sam hurried to his truck and made contact on his C.B. radio with a Challis base. He relayed the emergency message and asked for an ambulance. After giving the proper directions he returned to Pete and Amigo.

While they waited for the arrival of the ambulance, Pete told Sam the location of the camp and pick-up truck. He noted the keys had been left in the glove compartment. Pete then asked Sam to look after Amigo until he could come back for him and offered to pay for his keep.

Sam would have none of this and assured Pete everything would be safe and cared for.

He found a piece of paper and wrote his address and phone number on it. Then he placed the paper in Pete's shirt pocket.

"Don't worry Pete, I'll take care of everything and Amigo will be fine. We will be waiting for your return. Don't you worry none."

Within minutes the ambulance arrived and soon Pete was on his way to a hospital somewhere in Boise. Although he wasn't sure if Amigo could see or hear him, Pete waved and spoke with determination.

"I'll be seeing you, fella. You be good 'til I come back."

Aware that Pete was leaving without him, Amigo began to bark and did his best to pull away from Sam. Sam immediately knelt down beside Amigo and gently stroked the big dog while speaking in a whisper. "Take it easy big fella. Take it easy, he'll come back soon."

Amigo accepted Sam's kindness and within moments he had calmed down. Sam had no trouble getting Amigo to follow him into the big logging truck. Since they would not be able to reach Pete's camp until the road could be cleared, they headed back towards Sam's home and family.

As soon as it became possible, Sam and his eldest son Steve, found Pete's camp and brought the pick-up with all the equipment back to Sam's home for safekeeping.

Twelve days later and after successful eye surgery, Pete with Amigo at his side were on their way to sunny Arizona.

Meanwhile, Pete had learned that the earthquake was the largest to hit the continental United States since 1959. The quake measured 7.3 on the Richter scale and lasted some 40 seconds. It was said the quake had even affected the frequency of eruptions of Old Faithful in Yellowstone National Park. In addition the earthquake dropped a valley floor seven feet and raised the highest mountain, Mt. Borah at least another foot.